Exercise
Book for
Joseph Nguyen's

Don't Believe Everything You Think

Practical Activities, Prompts and Reflections

Paul Maynard for
PGPress

Disclaimer Notice:

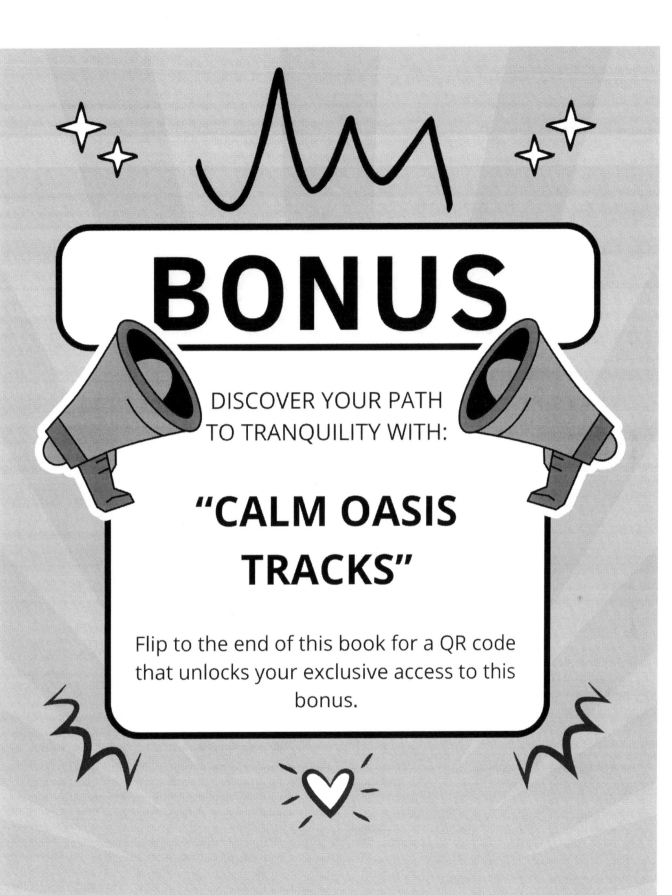

BONUS

DISCOVER YOUR PATH
TO TRANQUILITY WITH:

"CALM OASIS TRACKS"

Flip to the end of this book for a QR code that unlocks your exclusive access to this bonus.

Thank You!

I hope you will enjoy reading it as much as I enjoyed writing it. <u>Your support means the world to me!</u>

If you will find value in these pages, I kindly ask you to consider **leaving an honest review on Amazon.** Your feedback not only helps me improve but also helps other readers discover this book.

TABLE OF CONTENTS

Welcome to Your Journey of Self-Discovery

I'm here to introduce you to a workbook designed to accompany you as you delve into the profound pages of "Don't Believe Everything You Think." If you've ever wondered about the silent workings of your mind or questioned the intricate web of your thoughts, you're in the right place.

In this updated version, we've made some enhancements to ensure you have ample space for reflection, writing, and engaging in the exercises that will guide you along this path.

How to Use This Book

To get the most out of this exercise book, please take note of the following instructions:

Italics Text: Whenever you come across a text in italics, consider it a prompt. These prompts are designed to stir reflection, introspection, and personal insight. Take your time with these, allowing your thoughts and feelings to flow freely onto the pages provided.

> *Text in a Box: When you see text within a box, this signifies a more practical activity. These are hands-on exercises meant to bring the lessons into your daily life in tangible, actionable ways. Engage with these activities wholeheartedly, as they are key to integrating the book's teachings.*

Why an exercise book, You Ask?

Ever had an 'aha!' moment while reading and wished you had a way to capture that insight? That's what this workbook is all about. It's here to catch those fleeting thoughts and ground them in the soil of reflection and action.

A Step-by-Step Guide to Inner Clarity

You're not alone if you've ever found yourself lost in a maze of your thoughts. But what if I told you that each thought is a stepping stone to understanding the bigger picture of your life? This workbook is your map out of the maze. With each chapter corresponding to the original book's chapters, you'll find:

- Quick recaps to jog your memory and focus your thoughts.
- Simple, structured exercises that invite you to apply what you've learned.

- Prompt questions that aren't just about thinking but about doing and feeling.

Who's This For?

Whether you're a sage of self-reflection or just dipping your toes into the waters of personal growth, this exercise book is tailored for you. It's for anyone who's ever looked at their reflection and pondered, "What's next?"

Let's Talk Style

This isn't your typical textbook dialogue. Here, we're all about keeping it light, engaging, and oh-so-readable. You'll find sentences that dance and weave and others that get straight to the point. Why? Because that's how our minds work—full of contrasts and colors.

The Human Touch

Have you ever noticed how we're wired to respond to stories and examples? They're the lifeblood of learning. So, expect to find real-life scenarios sprinkled throughout, lighting up the path of insights with the warmth of shared experiences.

A Little Nudge of Encouragement

Ever heard the saying, "The proof is in the pudding"? Well, in the world of personal growth, the proof is in the doing. This workbook nudges you gently into action, with plenty of room to scribble, sketch, and see your growth unfold in real time.

A Final Thought

As we embark on this journey together, remember: this exercise book is a conversation, not a lecture. It's a dialogue between the wisdom of "Don't Believe Everything You Think" and the unique brilliance of your mind. So, let's begin, shall we? Flip the page, and let's turn thoughts into transformative action.

1: The Journey to Finding the Root Cause of Suffering

Chapter Overview

- The difference between pain and suffering: pain is inevitable; suffering is optional.
- The analogy of the two arrows: the first arrow is out of our control, and the second arrow is our reaction.
- The journey of self-improvement is often laden with trials, but understanding our minds can be our guide through the darkness.

Exercises and Reflections:

Identifying Your Arrows:

*Reflect on a recent painful event **and identify the 'second arrow'**—your reaction that may have compounded the pain into suffering. Write it down here.*

_____

_____

_____

_____

_____

_____

_____

_____

_____

_____

The Search for Solutions:

*Consider the myriad of solutions you have tried **to alleviate your suffering**. Which have brought temporary relief, and which have led to more confusion?*

Contemplation on Understanding:

*In a moment of quiet, think about what it would mean to **understand the workings of your mind**. How could this understanding transform your reaction to pain?*

Practical Application

Begin a daily practice of noting down painful events and your reactions. Look for patterns in how your 'second arrow' reactions may be adding to your suffering.

Experiment with one change this week in your routine that encourages mindfulness and awareness of your thought processes.

2: The Root Cause of All Suffering

Understanding the Origin of Our Inner Turmoil

Chapter Overview

- We live in a world shaped by our thoughts, not by objective reality.
- Our experiences and feelings are products of our interpretations.
- The meaning we assign to events dictates our emotional responses.
- Understanding that we can only feel what we think opens the door to changing our experience of life.

Exercises and Reflections:

The Coffee Shop Reflection:

*Picture yourself in a coffee shop. Write down two different scenarios of **how you perceive the environment**—one where you feel stressed and one where you feel content. Notice how your thoughts shape your experience.*

The Money Perspective:

What does money mean to you? *Jot down your thoughts and compare them with someone else's to see the diversity in perceptions.*

_____

_____

_____

_____

_____

_____

_____

Your Work, Your Thoughts:

*List the thoughts that **arise when you think about your job.** Now, imagine who you would be without those thoughts. Write down the emotions and states of being that emerge without your habitual thinking.*

_____

_____

_____

_____

_____

_____

Practical Application

Throughout the week, observe situations that normally trigger a negative response. Pause and ask yourself, "What am I thinking that's causing this feeling?" Aim to identify and write down the thought behind the emotion.

3: Why Do We Even Think?
Contemplating the Function of Thought

Chapter Overview

- Thinking has been a key element in human evolution, primarily for survival.
- The mind is adept at identifying potential dangers, often referencing past experiences.
- Understanding the mind's survival focus can prevent frustration and anger.
- Fulfillment and joy are the realms of consciousness and the soul, beyond mere survival.

Exercises and Reflections:

Survival vs. Thriving:

*Reflect on situations where your thinking was survival-oriented and compare them with times when your **thoughts were focused on joy and fulfillment.** Note the differences here.*

The Mind's Predictions:

*Recall a recent instance where your mind created **a hypothetical scenario based on memories.** Write down how this affected your emotions and compare it with the actual outcome.*

Beyond the Mind's Duty:

*Contemplate areas in your life where you've **allowed your mind to dictate your state of being.** How can tuning into your consciousness and soul alter this state?*

Practical Application

Practice mindfulness by identifying moments when you're in a fight or flight response. Pause and ask yourself, "Is this a true threat or just my mind's prediction?" Record your observations and any shifts in emotion.

Chapter 4: Thoughts vs. Thinking
Navigating the Landscape of Our Inner Dialogue

Chapter Overview

- Thoughts are effortless and arise from the Universe, beyond our control.
- Thinking is an active process that involves engaging with our thoughts, often leading to psychological suffering.
- Positive thoughts are a natural state of being, not a product of active thinking.
- The emotional weight of thinking can be heavy and restrictive, while pure thoughts feel light and expansive.

Exercises and Reflections:

The Thought Awareness Exercise:

Take a moment to sit quietly. Let thoughts arise and note them without engaging. Observe the difference between having a thought and beginning to think about it.

The Dream Income Visualization:

*Visualize the amount of **money you wish to make.** Write it down. Then multiply that by five and notice any changes in your emotional state. Reflect on this experience and the power of your engaged thinking.*

Thoughts vs. Thinking Chart:

Using the chart provided, identify moments from your day where you experienced 'Thoughts' versus 'Thinking'. Reflect on how each felt and what it led to in terms of your emotional state.

Attribute	Thought	Thinking
Source	Universe	Ego
Weight	Light	Heavy
Energy	Expansive	Restrictive
Nature	Infinite	Limited
Quality	Creative	Destructive
Charge	Positive	Negative
Essence	Divine	Mortal
Feeling	Alive	Stressful
Emotion	Love	Fear
Belief	Infinite Possibilities	Confining
Sense	Wholeness	Separateness
Effort	Effortless	Laborious

Practical Application

Practice pausing throughout the day to differentiate between spontaneous thoughts and active thinking. Try to embrace thoughts without slipping into the judgment or criticism that characterizes thinking.

Chapter 5: If We Can Only Feel What We're Thinking, Don't We Need to Think Positively to Feel That Way?

Unraveling the Myth of Positive Thinking

Chapter Insights:

- Negative emotions are often linked to our thinking, serving a survival function but not necessarily contributing to our happiness.
- Positive emotions do not require active thinking; they are reflective of our natural state of being, which is inherently filled with joy, love, and peace.
- The intensity of our emotions is inversely proportional to the amount of thinking we engage in; less thinking leads to stronger positive emotions.

Exercises and Reflections:

Joy and Love Recall Exercise:

*Reflect on a moment of **intense joy and love in your life.** Were you actively thinking during this moment, or were you simply experiencing the emotion? Document your observations and feelings.*

Thought Experiment on Stress vs. Happiness:

*Compare two memories: one where you felt **extremely stressed** and another where you experienced **profound happiness.** Note the level of thinking in each scenario and how it influenced your emotional state.*

Thought-o-Meter Visualization:

Imagine your mind has a "thought-o-meter" showing thoughts per minute. Visualize moments when this meter would rise into the red zone due to excessive thinking, leading to negative emotions. Contrast this with moments of low thinking and high positive emotion.

Practical Application:

Practice mindfulness by observing moments when your thinking intensifies and leads to stress. Use this awareness to consciously reduce your engagement with these thoughts, creating space for natural positive emotions to emerge.

Note:

Chapter 6: How the Human Experience Is Created - The Three Principles

Chapter Insights:

Universal Mind:
- Represents the intelligence and life force present in all living things.
- It is the source of our thoughts and the underlying connection between all elements in the universe, promoting feelings of wholeness, love, and peace.

Universal Consciousness:
- It serves as the collective awareness of all beings, enabling us to recognize our existence and be conscious of our thoughts.
- Acts as the medium through which we experience the world through our senses.

Universal Thought:
- The creative material from which we shape our reality, allows us to bring ideas and forms into existence.
- Functions as the content we become aware of, much like a movie brought to life through the combined efforts of a DVD, player, and electricity.

Exercises and Reflections:

Connection with Universal Mind Meditation:

*Spend a few moments in quiet reflection or meditation, focusing on **the sensation of being part of a larger, interconnected universe.** Reflect on any feelings of peace or insight that arise.*

Consciousness Awareness Practice:

*Throughout your day, periodically pause to observe your surroundings and experiences **through your senses.** Note these observations and how they make you feel, recognizing the role of consciousness in shaping these experiences.*

Creative Thought Visualization:

*Visualize an **idea or project you wish to bring to life.** Imagine this thought as a seed, your consciousness as the soil, and the Universal Mind as the sunlight and water nurturing its growth. Journal about this visualization and the feelings it evokes.*

Practical Application:

Integrate these principles into daily life by recognizing moments when you feel disconnected or negative. Use this awareness to remind yourself of your inherent connection to the Universal Mind, the role of your consciousness in shaping your experience, and the power of your thoughts to create your reality.

Chapter 7: If Thinking is the Root Cause of Our Suffering, How Do We Stop Thinking?

Chapter Insights:

- **Understanding the Zen Parable:** The chapter opens with a Zen parable illustrating the nature of heaven and hell, demonstrating how our reactions and thinking create our emotional realities.
- **Reducing Thinking:** It clarifies that completely stopping thinking isn't the goal but minimizing engagement with our thoughts to live more in the present moment.
- **Awareness:** Emphasizes the importance of awareness in minimizing thinking. By simply noticing that we're thinking, we can detach and allow thoughts to settle.

Exercises and Reflections:

The Water Bowl Meditation:

- *Exercise:* Observe a bowl of cloudy water and watch as the sediment settles over time. Reflect on how this **mirrors the process of thoughts settling** in your mind when left undisturbed.
- *Reflection:* How does recognizing the natural settling of your thoughts change your approach to managing stressful thinking?

Heaven and Hell Reflection:

Exercise: *Reflect on a recent situation where your reaction created a 'hellish' experience. How could a* **change in perception** *have created a 'heavenly' state instead?*

Reflection: *Consider the power of your reactions and how they shape your emotional reality.*

Quicksand Analogy Application:

Exercise: Next time you find yourself overthinking, pause and visualize yourself in quicksand. Remember, **struggling less means sinking less.** Apply this by consciously choosing to reduce your mental struggle.

Reflection: Note the differences in your emotional state when you choose not to engage with every thought that arises.

Practical Application:

Daily Awareness Practice: Throughout your day, periodically check in with your thoughts. Use the awareness of 'thinking' as a cue to return to the present moment, reducing engagement with unhelpful thought patterns.

Note:

Chapter 8: How Can We Possibly Thrive in the World Without Thinking?

Insights on Non-Thinking and Peak Performance

Chapter Insights:

- **State of Flow:** Engaging in work or activities that captivate us so fully that we lose all sense of time and self, entering a state of flow where thinking is minimal.
- **Peak Performance:** High-performing individuals, like Olympic athletes, operate in the zone or mushin—a state of mind free from cluttered thoughts, ego, anger, and fear, allowing for instinctive and intuitive action.
- **Mushin:** A Japanese concept describing a state of mind free from thoughts, emotions, and ego, enabling individuals to respond and act without hesitation based on training and instinct.

Exercises and Reflections:

Flow State Recall:

Reflect on a recent experience where you were completely absorbed in an activity. **What thoughts, if any, were going through your mind?** *Document how this state felt and the impact on your performance or enjoyment of the activity.*

Exploring Mushin:

Choose a simple task or activity you enjoy. **Engage in this activity to clear your mind** *of active thoughts, focusing solely on the action itself. Note any differences in your experience or performance.*

Thought Observation Exercise:

*Throughout your day, observe moments when **you find yourself in a natural flow** state versus when you are caught up in active thinking. Reflect on the quality of your actions and feelings in these different states.*

Practical Application:

Experiment with entering a state of non-thinking during various activities to explore how it affects your creativity, enjoyment, and performance. Use mindfulness or meditation techniques to help quiet the mind and access this state more readily.

Chapter 9: If We Stop Thinking, What Do We Do About Our Goals, Dreams & Ambitions?

Chapter Insights:

- Differentiating between goals born of inspiration versus those from desperation.
- Recognizing that our best, most fulfilling goals emerge not from a place of thinking and analyzing but from a deeper, intuitive understanding.
- Understanding that true inspiration for our goals and dreams bypasses conventional thinking and taps into a universal source of creativity and potential.

Exercises and Reflections:

Inspiration vs. Desperation Analysis:

*Reflect on your current goals and categorize them as **inspired by either desperation or inspiration.** Consider how this distinction affects your feelings and approach toward achieving these goals.*

Divine Inspiration Inquiry:

Ask yourself: ***"If I had infinite resources and no fear of failure, what would I choose to do?"*** *Allow answers to surface without engaging in analytical thinking. Note any insights or new goals that feel aligned with this exercise.*

Applying Insights:

Shift your focus from achieving goals as a means to an end (desperation) to engaging in activities that resonate with your core desires and bring intrinsic joy and fulfillment (inspiration).

Practice mindfulness to distinguish between the compulsive need to think through every detail of your goals and allowing a more spontaneous, inspired approach to guide your actions.

Note:

Chapter 10: Unconditional Love & Creation

Exploring the Essence of Unconditional Love and Creation

Core Concepts:

- **Unconditional Love:** Love without reasons, conditions, or boundaries. It's an outpouring of love that doesn't depend on external circumstances or specific traits/actions of others.
- **Unconditional Creation:** The purest form of creation, stemming not from a desire to achieve something else but from the joy of creation itself. It is innovative, unique, and often revolutionary, motivated by an internal drive rather than external goals.

Exercises and Reflections:

Reflecting on Unconditional Love:

*Consider a relationship or connection where **you feel love unconditionally**. Reflect on the nature of this love—how it feels, what it teaches you about yourself and love in general.*

Exploring Unconditional Creation:

*Engage in a creative activity **without any goal other than the activity itself.** It could be drawing, writing, singing, or any form of creation. Notice how this free form of creation feels compared to goal-oriented activities.*

Identifying Conditional vs. Unconditional Goals:

List your current goals and dreams. Categorize them into those created out of desperation (conditional) and those stemming from inspiration (unconditional). Reflect on how each category makes you feel and the driving force behind them.

Practical Application:

Practice creating from a place of abundance rather than lack. Whenever starting a new project or goal, ask yourself if it's motivated by unconditional love and creativity or if it's aiming to fulfill an external desire.

Reflective Questions:

- *How does the concept of unconditional love change your perspective on relationships and self-love?*
- *In what ways can you incorporate unconditional creation into your daily life to enhance your sense of fulfillment and connection to your true self?*

Chapter 11: What Do You Do Next After Experiencing Peace, Joy, Love & Fulfillment in the Present?

Directing Freed Energy Towards Inspired Goals

The cessation of constant thinking liberates a significant amount of energy previously consumed by stress and anxiety. The challenge and opportunity lie in redirecting this energy towards pursuits that are inspired rather than born out of desperation or anxiety.

Exercises and Reflections:

Identifying Inspired Goals:

Reflect on what truly inspires you. *These goals should feel light and energizing, coming from a place of abundance and desire to create for the sake of creation, not from a need or lack.*

Creating an Activation Ritual:

Develop a morning routine that sets the tone for a day of non-thinking and flow. This could include meditation, journaling, exercise, or any activity that centers you in your state of peace.

Channeling Energy Constructively:

Whenever you find yourself with excess energy or at a loose end, consciously choose activities that align with your inspired goals. Notice how this shifts your experience from one of aimlessness to one of purposeful creation.

Practical Application:

- *Make a list of inspired goals that genuinely excite you, devoid of any external pressures or expectations.*

- *Design your activation ritual. Experiment with different activities to find what best helps you maintain your state of non-thinking throughout the day.*

- *When you catch yourself slipping into old patterns of overthinking, gently remind yourself of your inspired goals and direct your energy towards them.*

Note:

Chapter 12: Nothing Is Either Good or Bad

Exploring the Nature of Judgment and Perception

Key Insights:

- The analogy of a piano's 88 keys illustrates that, like the notes which are not inherently wrong, decisions in life are not inherently good or bad; it's our perception that determines their value.
- The concept extends to all aspects of life, including political views, personal decisions, and interactions, suggesting a move away from dualistic thinking (right/wrong, good/bad) towards seeking universal truths.
- True truth is universal and non-subjective, found within oneself rather than through external validation or reasoning.

Exercises and Reflections:

Perception Shift Exercise:

*Identify a situation in your life **that you've labeled as "bad" or "wrong."** Reflect on the underlying thoughts and perceptions that led to this label. Consider alternative perspectives or truths that might change your perception.*

Universal Truths Exploration:

*Spend some time in contemplation or meditation, **seeking a universal truth that resonates** deeply with you. It could be related to the nature of love, peace, or interconnectedness. Reflect on how this truth influences your perception of events in your life.*

Emotional Awareness Practice:

*Next time you find yourself experiencing strong negative emotions, pause and acknowledge that **these emotions stem from your thinking**. Approach your thoughts with curiosity rather than judgment, allowing them to dissipate and return you to a state of peace.*

Applying Insights:

Instead of categorizing experiences or people's actions as good or bad, strive to understand the underlying truths and perspectives. This approach fosters empathy, openness, and a deeper connection to the universal truths that bind us.

Note:

Chapter 13: How Do You Know What to Do Without Thinking?

Embracing Intuition and Inner Wisdom

Key Insights:

- **Trust in Intuition:** The importance of relying on our gut feeling or intuition, which serves as an inner GPS, guiding us through life's decisions with real-time advice.
- **Inner Wisdom:** Acknowledges that deep down, we often know what to do in various situations but may be held back by fear, doubt, or societal pressures.
- **The Role of Fear and Self-Doubt:** Identifies fear and self-doubt as major obstacles that prevent us from accessing our inner knowledge and intuition.

Exercises and Reflections:

Intuition Awareness Exercise:

*Spend a day consciously noting moments when you **feel an intuitive nudge about a decision or action.** Reflect on how following or ignoring these nudges affects the outcome and your emotional state.*

Identifying Fear and Self-Doubt:

*Write down a decision you're **currently struggling with.** List the fears or doubts that come up when you think about this decision. Ask yourself if these fears are based on thinking patterns that you can acknowledge and release.*

Trust-Building Exercise:

*Choose a small, low-stakes decision to make **based solely on your intuition.** Reflect on the process and the outcome. Did trusting your intuition lead to a positive result? How did it feel to rely on your inner guidance?*

Practical Application:

Work on recognizing and distinguishing between your intuitive insights and the noise created by overthinking. Practice pausing and tuning into your gut feeling before making decisions.

Embracing Non-Thinking Decision Making:

Understand that not knowing what to do at times is okay and that the clarity often comes from a place of non-thinking. Trust that your inner wisdom will provide the guidance you need when the time is right.

Chapter 14: How to Follow Your Intuition

Key Points:

- Intuition connects us directly to a state of non-thinking or flow, aligning us with the universe or God.
- Non-thinking allows access to inner wisdom, enabling decision-making without the stress of analysis.
- True intuition comes without the need for external validation, often going against logical reasoning.
- Following intuition can lead to unexpected and miraculous outcomes, guiding us through life effortlessly.

Exercises and Reflections:

Identify Intuitive Moments:

*Reflect on past decisions where **you followed your intuition.** Note the outcome and how you felt during the process. This exercise aims to increase trust in your intuitive insights.*

Intuition vs. Fear:

When facing a decision, note your initial gut feeling versus the thoughts that follow. This practice helps differentiate between intuitive guidance and fear-based thinking.

Daily Intuition Journal:

Keep a journal to record instances where you feel a strong intuitive pull. Documenting these moments can enhance your awareness and trust in your intuition.

Practical Application:

Practice mindfulness to stay present, the state where intuition is most accessible.

Use meditation or quiet reflection to calm the mind, allowing your intuition to speak more clearly.

Act on small intuitive impulses to build confidence in your inner guidance system, gradually trusting it for more significant life decisions.

Chapter 15: Creating Space for Miracles

Key Insights:

- **Space for Creation:** Just as the universe emerged from nothingness, our minds also require emptiness to foster new thoughts and ideas. This chapter emphasizes the importance of creating mental space to allow for the manifestation of miracles.
- **Non-Thinking as a Tool:** The practice of non-thinking is highlighted as a method to clear the mind, akin to emptying a cup, to make room for new insights and solutions to emerge spontaneously.
- **Historical Examples:** Stories of renowned individuals like Thomas Edison and Albert Einstein illustrate how stepping away from active problem-solving to engage in rest or unrelated activities can facilitate creative breakthroughs and solutions.

Exercises and Reflections:

Empty Your Cup Exercise:

*Reflect on areas of your life where **your mind feels overly full or cluttered.** Commit to a period of non-thinking, perhaps through meditation or a quiet walk, to clear this mental space.*

Question for Space Creation:

Ask yourself challenging questions that disrupt your usual pattern of thinking. This can create gaps in your thought process, making room for new ideas.

Activation Ritual:

Develop a morning or daily ritual that encourages a state of flow and non-thinking, such as playing an instrument, engaging in a hobby, or simply sitting in silence.

Practical Application:

When faced with challenges, instead of immediately trying to think your way out, allow yourself to step back and create mental space. Trust that the solution will emerge from this space of non-thinking.

Note:

Chapter 16: What Happens When You Begin Living in Non-Thinking (Potential Obstacles)

Key points

- **Unfamiliar Peace:** Initially, the profound sense of peace and serenity you discover through non-thinking may feel unfamiliar or unsettling. Our inherent resistance to the unfamiliar might trick us into believing something is amiss when, in fact, we are experiencing true peace.

- **Fear of Lost Productivity:** There's a common misconception that non-thinking leads to decreased productivity, a loss of competitive edge, or laziness. Contrary to this belief, non-thinking often enhances productivity, creativity, and personal magnetism, attracting more opportunities and positive outcomes.

- **The Importance of Faith:** Faith plays a crucial role in navigating the journey of non-thinking. Trusting that the universe is conspiring in your favor, that every experience serves a purpose, and that embracing the unknown opens the door to limitless possibilities is essential.

- **Battling the Mind's Resistance:** Your mind might attempt to revert to old patterns of thinking, convincing you that peace and happiness are signs of something being wrong. Recognizing this as a tactic to draw you back into unnecessary thinking is key to maintaining your newfound state of bliss.

- **Handling Relapses into Thinking:** Should you find yourself slipping back into old thinking patterns, approach this with kindness and understanding towards yourself. It's a natural part of the human experience. Recognizing that your thoughts are the source of discomfort allows you to return to a state of peace effortlessly.

Strategies for Overcoming Obstacles:

- **Maintain Faith:** Keep faith in the unseen and the unknown. Understand that true change and miracles lie beyond the familiar.

- **Acknowledge and Release:** When you notice thoughts creeping in, simply acknowledge their presence without judgment and gently let them go, returning to your state of non-thinking.

- **Cultivate an Inner Compass:** Trust your intuition and inner wisdom to guide you through life's decisions without overthinking.

- **Embrace the Present:** Focus on remaining in the present moment, where peace, joy, and love naturally reside.

Chapter 17: Now What?

Key Points:

- **Continuous Journey:** The chapter emphasizes that the end of the book marks the beginning of a new phase of life for the reader, one where peace, love, and joy are accessible through non-thinking.
- **The simplicity of Truth:** It highlights the simplicity of truth, cautioning readers against complicating their path to peace with unnecessary thinking and complexity.
- **Inner Wisdom:** The importance of listening to one's inner wisdom is underscored, guiding readers to trust in their soul and inner guidance rather than external influences and opinions.
- **State of Being:** It reaffirms that everything one needs and desires — love, joy, peace, fulfillment — is already within, obscured only by the clutter of thought.
- **Miracles of Non-Thinking:** By living in a state of non-thinking, readers are encouraged to expect miracles and transformations in their lives, becoming beacons of love and joy to those around them.

Note:

A Guide to Stop Thinking
Exercises:

Minimize Thinking Triggers:

List actions or environments that trigger overthinking or stress. Aim to reduce or eliminate these from your daily life.

Cultivate Inspiring Activities:

Identify and engage in activities that excite and inspire you, creating a conducive environment for non-thinking.

Morning Activation Ritual:

Develop a morning ritual that starts your day in a peaceful, non-thinking state. Incorporate activities like meditation, journaling, or yoga that connect you with Infinite Intelligence.

Daily Decompression:

Schedule time for activities that help you relax and return to a state of non-thinking, such as taking a walk, meditating, or playing with pets.

Note:

Framework For How To Stop Thinking

Steps:

1. Acknowledge Thinking as the Root Cause:

Recognize when suffering occurs, it's a result of thinking. Differentiate between involuntary thoughts and active thinking.

2. Allow Space for Negative Thinking:

Acknowledge and allow negative thoughts without resistance, understanding they are not the essence of who you are.

3. Transition to Positive Emotions:

Once acknowledged, let the thoughts pass. If negative feelings persist, revisit step one.

Note:

Potential Obstacles
Challenges and Solutions:

Attachment to Thinking:

Understand that past methods won't always lead to new results. Embrace non-thinking for happiness and productivity.

Lack of Faith:

Cultivate belief in the possibility of a life filled with joy, peace, and love by trusting in a greater force.

Overcoming Fear:

Recognize fear as a sign of importance. Everything you desire is beyond fear. Use the framework to navigate through fear by stopping the cycle of thinking.

Note:

Reflection Prompts

1. *On a scale of 1-10, how much did you think today?*

2. *What percentage of your day was spent in a relaxed state versus fight or flight mode?*

Creating a Non-Thinking Environment
Framework:

1. Audit Thinking Triggers:

Identify what in your life leads to overthinking or stress. Categorize these triggers for better management.

2. Categorize and Prioritize:

Organize triggers by impact and start with modifying or removing the most affecting ones.

3. Activation Rituals:

Design a morning routine that sets a non-thinking tone for the day, integrating practices that connect you to your higher self.

4. Workplace Integration:

Identify work activities that energize versus drain you. Aim to spend 80% of your work time on energizing tasks.

5. Addressing Destructive Habits:

Acknowledge behaviors you wish to change. Understand the trigger feelings and thoughts, and consult your inner wisdom for insights to change.

Implementation Guide

1. Recognition and Willingness to Change:

Identify and accept the behavior you want to change.

2. Detailed Observation:

Note the frequency, triggers, and feelings associated with the behavior.

2. Understanding Triggers:

Dive deep into the emotions and thought patterns that trigger the behavior.

4.Insight and Release:

Seek insights from your inner wisdom on why and how to change, embracing the feelings of freedom and peace that follow.

NOTES:

About the Author

Paul Maynard stands at the forefront of educational innovation, embodying the essence of learning through engagement. As a distinguished member and writer for PG Press, Paul has dedicated his career to transforming the way we approach knowledge. His philosophy is simple yet profound: true understanding comes from an active dialogue with the material, not passive memorization. This belief is the cornerstone of his work, making each of his exercise books not just a tool for learning but a journey toward enlightenment.

Paul's expertise lies in breaking down complex concepts into digestible, engaging lessons that resonate with readers from all walks of life. His unique approach incorporates idiomatic expressions and real-world examples, ensuring that challenging ideas are not only grasped but retained. Through his work, Paul has redefined the table of contents from a mere list of headings to a comprehensive map that guides readers to moments of clarity and insight.

At the heart of Paul's methodology is the conviction that knowledge must be applicable to be valuable. He crafts his workbooks with the intent of not just imparting wisdom but enabling readers to apply what they learn in meaningful ways. His pages are meticulously designed with clarity in mind, utilizing bolded key points and italicized nuances to facilitate a deeper understanding of the subject matter.

Paul Maynard's contributions to PG Press and the educational landscape are immeasurable. His workbooks are more than educational resources; they are catalysts for personal and professional growth, empowering readers to not only acquire knowledge but to live it.

About PG Press

PG Press stands as a collective of workbook experts, united by a singular mission: to enhance the learning experience of readers worldwide. Our team is driven by the belief that the true value of reading lies in its ability to inspire action, provoke thought, and foster a deeper understanding of the world around us. We specialize in creating practical, useful, and meticulously planned workbooks that complement a wide array of subjects and interests.

At PG Press, we are more than just publishers; we are facilitators of knowledge, dedicated to offering our readers the tools they need to extract the maximum value from every book they explore. Our workbooks are designed to bridge the gap between theoretical knowledge and practical application, ensuring that every reader can find relevance and meaning in the pages.

Our commitment to quality and utility is reflected in every workbook we publish. With a keen eye for detail and a passion for learning, PG Press continues to set the standard for educational resources, empowering readers to unlock their potential, one page at a time.

Thank You!

I hope you enjoyed reading it as much as I enjoyed writing it. <u>Your support means the world to me!</u>

If you found value in these pages, I kindly ask you to consider **leaving an honest review on Amazon.** Your feedback not only helps me improve but also helps other readers discover this book.

Access your bonus content

Calm Oasis Tracks

Scan the QR code
or copy this link: **https://o2o.to/i/p8FQf3**

SCAN ME

...and enjoy!

Made in the USA
Las Vegas, NV
20 November 2024

12160471R00046